Wings of Courage

Written by: Janice Marie

Wings of Courage

Sharing My Journey of Adversity in Poetry

Janice Marie

WCP
Pearl S. Buck Writing Center Press
Perkasie, Pennsylvania

Author Note
My journey of adversity is conveyed from my perceptions as a child, adolescent, and young adult. I share my honest feelings and memory details to the best of my ability.

ISBN-13 #:9798642274118

First Edition

WCP

Pearl S. Buck Writing Center Press

520 Dublin Road, Perkasie, PA 18944

www.psbi.org/writingcenter

Janice Marie

WingsOfCourageJM@gmail.com

https://www.facebook.com/JaniceMarieWingsofCourage/

Wings of Courage

My first poetry collection is dedicated to my **amazing village!**

Sometimes life can leave us
speechless, afraid, and feeling ashamed.

Over the past twenty years, I have been
learning to find my way out of the darkness
that consumed my childhood and adolescence.

The journey has taken a village of loved ones
to help me soar with confidence and hope each morning.

I dedicate this collection of poems to my amazing village
of remarkable individuals and to Jesus, my Lord,
who blessed me with the gift of healing by writing poetry.

Table of Contents

Broken

My Inside Out

In a classroom of children, I feel alone.
In a school where Monster walks the halls, I feel afraid.
In a day of childhood bliss, I feel dismissed.

You all look at my weight and crack a joke.
You all look at my appearance and offer a rude evaluation.
You all think you know me from the outside in.

Do you want to walk in my shoes?
Do you want to face the Monster?
Do you want to shake in terror until exhaustion lets you sleep?

In a classroom of peers, long for my teacher to see me.
In a school where the Monster is known, I long to hide.
In a day of childhood bliss, I long for help to see this mess.

You all keep laughing at my size.
You all keep remarking on my less than popular looks.
You all keep thinking I'm weak and stupid.

I am stronger than you think.
I am braver than you believe.
I am resilient to your hurtful ways because I slay a Monster everyday!

Teachers became my rescuers.
Teachers became my safety.
Teachers became my voice.

In a classroom of children, I slip into the corner as a punching bag.
In a school where Monster walks, I slip into the "are you related to him" shame.
In a day of childhood bliss, I slip into daydreams of happiness.

My world seems unfair.
My voice seems useless.
My body seems unsatisfactory.
My family seems unusual.
My world seems unfamiliar to all who know my name.

In a classroom of children, I AM trapped.
In a school where Monster walks, I AM scared.
In a day of childhood bliss, I AM emptiness .

Will someone hear my cries?
Will someone stop the bullies?
Will someone protect my soul?
Will someone care if I stay in the hole?
Will someone rescue me from the Monster?
Will someone listen to my silent screams?

In a classroom of others, I dream of being acknowledged.
In a school where Monster walks the halls, I dream of him leaving.
In a day of childhood bliss, I dream of not being abused and neglected.

One day you might value me from the inside out and not judge me from the outside in.
One day I will rise above the darkness.
One day Monster will be caged.
One day...
One day...
One day...
Will it ever come?

Now I wait for help,
Now I numb to endure,
Now I pray, I'll survive for all to see me from the inside out!

Hardwood Floors

Hardwood floors covered the house.
Hardwood floors made Monster's footsteps frightening .
Hardwood floors made my bare body sore.

No room in the house was off limits.
No adult was around.
No knock was allowed to be ignored.
Monster knew he would never be found.

Hardwood floors broke my falls.
Hardwood floors absorbed all my tears.
Hardwood floors felt all my fears.

Privacy null and void.
Privacy made Monster hungry.
Privacy never found a safe door.
Monster had access to all of me like he was king of the country.

Hardwood floors listened to my endless pleas.
Hardwood floors wrapped me like a blanket in the darkness of evil.
Hardwood floors needed a secret door.

Monster pinned me down on hardwood floors for years.
Monster bruised my quivering body with pride.
Monster silenced my voice with his twisted lies.
Who am I that I belonged to Monster?

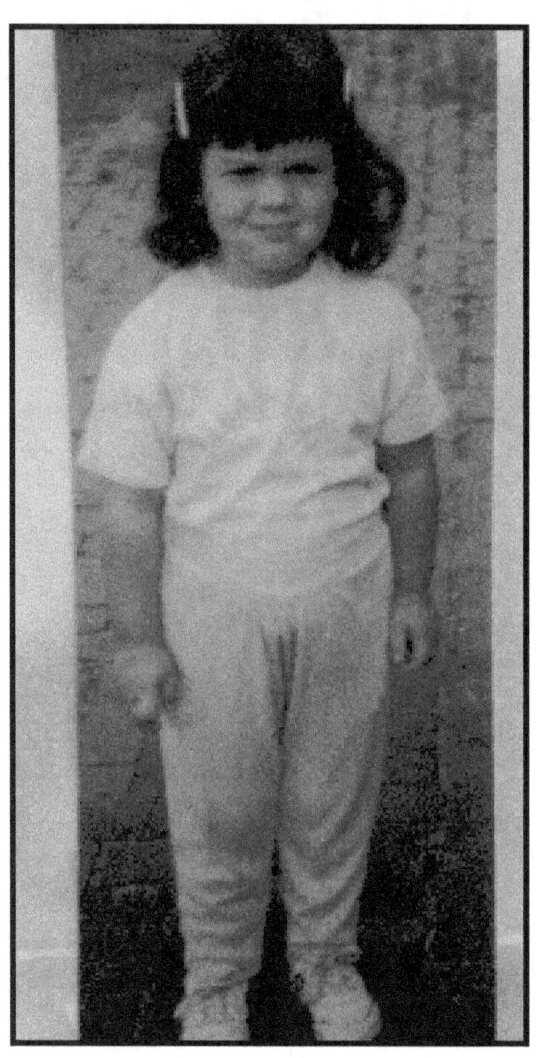

My little Janice Marie before she encountered the monster.

My kindergarten school year.

My Dearest Child

My dearest child, *WAKE UP*.

I am all around you. Do not weep.

I am here on solid ground.

Listen to the sounds that resound in your heart time and time again.

It has been me, your Daddy in Heaven.

I have been speaking to you, my dearest child. Have you not heard me?

I see you seeking for help in this battle, but you do not come to me.

You give up halfway and fall back asleep, praying it will go away.

I am here to stay!

I have been watching over you through all the nights you have turned around.

My Dearest Child, **WAKE UP**!

I want to hold you tight.

All you have to do is let go and reach to the highest of heights.

The gates to my house have been forever opened wide for **you**.

Come home and hide from the overwhelming fight that you do not have the might to calm.

It is not greed needing me constantly.

It is here in My palm that you belong, my dearest child, for eternity!

The sighs you cry at night make my heart heavy.

Let me, your Daddy in Heaven, carry you all of your days, my dearest child!

In me your finest dreams will come true!

In me is where the freedom you long for can be found!

My dearest child, Please Come home!

I love you!

My Grandmother proudly watched me blow out my 5th birthday candles.
She set an amazing example of courage and strength!

I am in awe of how my birthday wishes have been answered,
by Jesus, in the most unexpected ways.

My Best Friend

My world changed the day four paws
met my stride step for step.
She became the greatest companion and never left my side.

Many called her Patches,
I will always call her *my best friend.*

My lonely days with Monster seemed more bearable with
Patches step for step.
She endured my silent screams and never left my side.

Many called her Patches,
I will always call her *my protector.*

My stomach twisted with fear as I tried to hide with Patches night after night.
She rested her head on me and licked my salty tears.

Many called her Patches,
I will always call her *my secret keeper.*

My heart began to feel loved with her tender affection night after night.
She helped me survive the terrors raging within the brick walls.

Many called her Patches,
I will always call her *My Best Friend.*

Her eyes could speak to my wounded soul.
Her soft coat could sooth my trembling body.
Her gentle spirit could bring peace to my weary mind.

My world changed the day her four paws met my stride step for step.
I clung to her until her final breath.
I love you forever.
I feel you are always near.
You saved my life and blessed me beyond measure!

My best friend - My Patches !
My world of light in years of darkness .
My beloved dog - My best friend !

Animals have a wonderful way of helping us face the heartaches of life.
What animal has seen you through to the other side of despair?

FREEDOM

Here I stand, singing with the band.

I raise my hand, praying for freedom.

I want to be in your kingdom when my life on Earth is said and done.

But my heart weighs a ton and I'm bound behind a gun watching others have fun.

How can I let your Son hold me tight throughout this fight?

Only my sight keeps me dreaming about knowing your love and freedom even in the night.

I see your light in a candle before my face.

Let me feel your GRACE before I race back to the wounds my mind and soul taste and know

as home base.

I need your strength to chase away the lies and courage to give you my life so I can live in

your freedom.

I'm alive.

I'm alive.

I'm alive!

As I strive to feel your hand, as I sing with the band,
Here in your land,
I want FREEDOM!!!

believe

Speak

Let It Out

Pacing.
My heart is racing.
My fears I'm facing.
Pacing.

I am,
Searching for the words to say,
Praying for the strength to speak,
Looking for the comfort to heal.

Pacing.
My hands reach for my phone.
My secret keeps me feeling alone.
My life is about to reach an unwanted milestone.
Pacing.

I'm here!
What's going on?
I'm here!
Are you ready for this?
I'm here with you!

Pacing.
My thoughts are confusing me.
My truth is going to be set free.
My pain they must finally see.
Pacing.

Breathe!
I won't hang up until you tell me it's okay.
Breathe!
You can let this out and face them finally.
Breathe!
Rip off the band-aid and let IT out.
Breathe!

It's time!
Parents are home - I have to go.
It's time!

Frozen!
I mumble my urgency to speak.
I stutter my way through the proof and feel weak.
I collapse to the floor when they freak.
Frozen!

I let **IT** out.
I am paralyzed as they look at me and shout.
I am blamed for my secrets and I want to blackout.
I let **IT** out!

Abandoned.
I packed my bags.
I was left on a doorstep.
IT was my parents' treasure and I feel like I am their rags.
I lost everything and more when I let **IT** out.
Abandoned.

Weeping.
I am shameful.
I am disgusted.
I am unwanted.
Weeping.

I let IT out
I let IT out
I LET IT OUT!

Abuse won't choke me to the core anymore
Abuse won't be hidden- I've opened the door
Abuse won't win - I will find my **ROAR**

Pacing.
My heart is still racing.
My dreams I will be chasing.
My friends I will be embracing.
Pacing!

*Thank you , my friend,
for helping me slay a giant and for answering
my phone call on this dark night. *

Where is My Home

Dark clouds hover over every step I take.
I dream of having a HOME to battle the storm.
Isolation plagues my will to survive.
I dream of having a HOME to feel safe.

How do I stand?
How do I speak?
How do I succeed?

I'm broken and crumbled under this smile.
I'm trampled into the ground by fear.
HOME - I need you!
HOME - why don't I deserve you?
HOME - will I ever know the gift of a you?

I'm slipping away day by day.
I'm unsure how to pray.
I'm searching for a way to stay and win the day.

My child you are always in My HOME!
My child lift your eyes to the heavens.
My child reach for My hand.

I Am standing with you!
I Am speaking to you!
I Am helping you succeed!

A house is a building but a HOME is always within you.
A house is not forever.
A HOME never abandons you.
A house hides traumas never meant for you to endure.
A HOME is love as I Am LOVE!

HOME is the love You feel from My presence in your life,
HOME is the photographs in your mind of our sweet memories,
HOME is the protected corner of your heart no one can take from you,
HOME will always be within your soul.

Trust in the beauty of our HOME.
Let go of the house that destroyed you.
Believe in the power of our HOME to heal.
Let go of the house that silenced you.
Hold on to the HOME of My love.
Let go of the house that failed you.to
Embrace our HOME and all its graces.

Welcome HOME my child!
You are loved!
You are not forgotten!
You are mine!
You are worth more than you can imagine!
HOME is within you!

Please come HOME!
I'm here!
I'm waiting for you, *my beloved child*!

Lost in thought over the Pacific Ocean in Oregon.

REWIND

I can't believe I said this,
REWIND this, Jesus.
Please, I can't handle the chaos,
REWIND this, Jesus.
Please, I can't handle being rejected,
REWIND this, Jesus.
Please, I can't handle being exposed,
REWIND my life, Jesus.
Please, Please take me away!

Why do I feel like they will never care?
They blame me for my despair.
They turned their backs and walked separate roads.
I'm left alone to repair!

They could only freak.
They would not let my wounds leak.
They feared my truth would tarnish their names.
I'm an adult learning to REWIND, so I can undo the lies and freely speak.

Jesus,
I know you are always at my side.
I know you have carried me all these years.
I know you are all I need.
I know you LOVE me.

My secret is out.
I can't REWIND!
My heart is broken as they shout.
I can't REWIND!
My world is forever changed.
I can't REWIND!
I need to learn this walk, this new chapter.
I can't REWIND!

Jesus,
Please bring my mind peace.
Please heal what I can't REWIND!

Once I overcame the shock of people knowing my truth,

I found beautiful freedom in letting my truth bloom like a flower!

I Am With You

My child,

My precious child,

<u>I Am with you!</u>

Silence the words others speak to you.

Hear My truth over their empty roar.

Close your eyes to the visions others give you.

Trust My promise that I hear the desires of your heart.

My child,

My sweet child,

<u>I Am still with you!</u>

Others will knock you down.

I will lift you up.

Others will break your heart.

I will mold the pieces back together again!

My child,

My dearest child,

<u>I Am never leaving you.</u>

This world is filled with doubt and fear.

My Word is filled with wisdom and hope.

This world is dark and broken.

My Love is perfect and pure.

My child,

My **tender** child,

<u>I Am always with you!</u>

Help this world know My name.

Share My love with everyone you meet.

Give my grace unconditionally.

Be My gift to this broken world.

My child,

My **beloved** child,

<u>Together is where we belong!</u>

<u>Crayon Dreams</u>

Blank paper holds endless possibilities for crayons to create my passions with my little fingers.
My innocent young eyes perfectly color the longings deep within my heart and soul.
Lines and colors orchestrate my vivid crayon dreams of what will happen when I grow up.

A bride walking down the aisle with her daddy!
A mother holding her beautiful babies!
A teacher to young children in my elementary school!
A house filled with endless love and peace!

Daily my gaze lingers at my crayon dreams and I pray today will be the day one comes true.
As promising as waves will crash along the shore,
Time keeps passing and waiting makes my crayon dreams slowly fade.
Fear and doubt hover over my crayon dreams and whisper I don't matter to Him above.
My heart cries out WHY is my life not going like I dreamed for so many years.

Let me transform your crayon dreams and be the artist of your life.
I know what is BEST for you, my daughter.
This world tarnishes your innocence and sets false measures of
success - don't grow weary of worldly failures, my daughter.
I have blessings abound prepared for you in my perfectly painted
picture... trust In Me and know I know the desires of your heart.

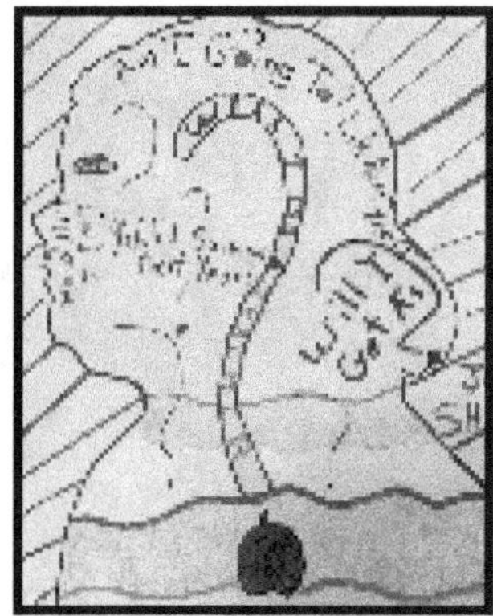

My 6th grade art project

You will never be alone and are **LOVED**.
You have "mothered" many beautiful children.
You are teaching children I need you to teach.
You have shelter from the storms of your life.
Don't give up my child.
Keep reaching for me my child.   .
Don't be afraid.
Keep striving to know me, my child.
Don't feel defeated.
Keep rising above the water.

Hand me your crayon dreams and fly into my heavens for your masterpiece of holy dreams.
Holy Spirit will lead you beyond any crayon dream that will fill your heart and soul abundantly!

As a child I often dreamed of seeing the world.
In 2013 I took my first trip to Europe and I love exploring new places!

FORWARD MOTION

Push and pull,
Back and forth,
Up and down,
Just to crash on the ground.

Life is not easy.
Life has no handbook.
Life is learning to keep forward motion.

Highs and lows,
Joys and sorrow,
Mountains and valleys,
Just to know emotions come back around.

Life can be painful.
Life can be unwanted situations.
Life can be demanding but keep forward motion.

Laughter and cries,
Hellos and farewells,
Beginnings and ends,
Just to hear life's array of sound.

Life will give you wings to soar.
Life will be your inner companion.
Life will be twists and turns as you keep forward motion.

Believe in the power of your dreams.
Believe in the gift your life has to offer.
Believe in the adventure with each forward step.

One step becomes two,
Two steps become three,
Every forward step leading you to who God called you to be!

Rise

A Child's Roar

A child's first cry is a precious gift never to be forgotten.
A life so real,
A baby so innocent,
A new story to be told.

A child's first injury is a pain that stops a mother's breath.
A time for tenderness,
A time for comfort,
A time for healing.

Where is the child's mother when the monster comes?

The child has their first heart battle scar.
Tears make a streamline to the floor,
Fears nestle in the pit of the child's stomach,
Curled in a ball trying to rock herself to sleep.

A child's first at bat as their parents cheer.
A time for clapping,
A time for joy,
A time for celebration.

A child's graduation puts delight in their father's eyes.
A life to be proud of,
A baby to reminisces,
A new story unfolding.

Where is the child's father when the monster comes?

The child, now grown, has their thousandth battle scar.
Tears make a pool for her feet to stand in,
Fears are punching her in the stomach,
Curled in a ball trying to rock herself to sleep.

I know the child.
I ache for the child.
I want to help the child.
I need to understand the child is ME!

A battle-scarred heart,
An ocean of tears to grieve,
Years of fears to be freed.

Lord, help me stand strong and brave for the child.
Lord, help me be tender to the child.
Lord, help me feel love for the child.

Swirling winds cover me.
The pit of my stomach is raging alive.
I stand and shake.
Here comes the earthquake.

I open and clench my fist.
I brace my body on unsinkable ground.
I open my mouth.

And let her ROAR!!!

A roar so painful.
A roar so hidden.
A roar so broken.
A roar so unspoken.

From the depths of my being, I let the child ROAR!

She falls into the arms of Jesus.
Sweet rest for His child.
The first cry He remembers,
The first wound He healed,
The first hit He cheered for,
The first graduation He was proud of,
The story of His child His child being **redeemed!!!**

Melting My Frozen Walls

My child's soul so free and bright,
A spirit of pure innocence and light,
Selfishly stolen for a male's delight,
I was too young to know I should fight.

He did not consider that my body was not to be shared.
He locked me in total isolation and froze my lips to conceal his secret,
my raging despair.

Frozen lips
      Frozen heart
            Frozen door

I can't let anyone in,
I can't let anyone know,
I can't let anyone see,
My icicle core because I'll be broken more.

Worthless
      Damaged
            Shattered

I try to find my way to melt the icicles.
With my silent screams echoing down the halls.
My parents are burdened by my weary calls.
Silence falls!

So long I've been the good girl to be the peacemaker,
So long I've pushed on without knowing how to stand,
So long I've been trapped forced to wear a brave face,
So long I've scrubbed my body trying to erase the wounds.

But my battle scars don't disappear,
Time will not erase all my fears,
Somehow I have to let go and feel the salty tears.

No turning back,
I've got to let go and let my icicles walls melt,
I don't want to die with the broken-hearted.

Lord Je**sus, do** you hear me?

I need you to cover me,
I need you to sit with me,
I need you to heal me,
I need you to teach me,
How to melt my icicle walls and make them flowing healing waters.
How to rebuild my shattered heart and broken dreams.
How to feel valued.

I want to be your cherished masterpiece!

I won't give up,
I won't let fear keep me down,
I want to run the distance!

I'm letting my icicle core melt.
It is **painful**.
It is *SCARY*.
It seems never-ending.

Help me find my voice.

Help me relinquish control.

Help me fight compulsive behaviors.

Help me feel worthy.

Help me feel whole.

Help me feel wanted.

Help me feel strong.

Help me feel radiant.

Help me feel peace.

Help me feel safe.

Help me feel alive.

Help me lift my eyes to You as Your loved and beautiful daughter.

By Your Grace, Jesus,

I have Faith that one day

I'll be set **FREE!!!**

Finding the courage
to allow my walls to melt
took many years.

I found a lot of support
in the musical
<u>The Color Purple.</u>

Learning to smile and take selfies also took time.
I found the strength to let myself
wear my hair down.

I allowed myself to embrace
the freedom of not living in fear.

The Lord's love is greater for me than the ocean is
deep
no matter what struggles I endure.

Breathe

Breaking the silence,

Responding positively to fears,

Echoing my voice of power,

Adapting to life - giving patterns,

Taking control with engaged thinking,

Holding my inner child with love,

Enduring triggers with peace and confidence!

Breathe, just keep breathing! Victory will come!!!

*Have you ever allowed yourself to pause and **breathe** in the gift of nature?*

After the loss of my beloved Grandmother, I found the gift of running.
I had spent most of my life on the sidelines longing to join the race.

Now I run the race step by step!
I have even completed a half marathon in Disneyland!

Rise Above The Hurt

A moment of pain
becomes
A day of hurt
becomes
A week of anger
becomes
A month of grief
becomes
Years of my life just slipping away

How do I smile?
How do I stand?
How do I even begin to BREATHE?

This is not the life I wanted
This is not the life I dreamed
This is not the way things are supposed to be
Years of my life are slipping away

How can I pray?
How can I sing?
How can I even BREATHE again?

A brick of fear
builds
A brick of anger
builds
A brick of sadness
builds
A brick of bitterness
builds
A brick of unforgiveness
builds
A WALL of insecurity and weakness

Why am I still here?
Why am I all alone?
Why won't YOU let this go away?

RISE above your pain!

Be Brave!

RISE!

It is time to exchange your baggage for gifts
One by one
Hand me your brick of fear
You HAVE peace
Hand me your brick of anger
You HAVE passion
Hand me your brick of sadness
You HAVE comfort
Hand me your brick of bitterness
You HAVE compassion
Hand me your brick of unforgiveness
You HAVE love

RISE above your doubt!

Be Brave!

RISE!

I am working to heal all your wounds
I am molding your heart to fully know mine
I am building your strength to fight all of life's battles
I am restoring your life with strength from your
beautiful scars
I am always LOVING you unconditionally

RISE above the ashes!

Be Transformed!

RISE and surrender!

Be *My Precious Warrior*!

RISE!

You are **STRONGER!**

You are **LOVED!**

You are **WORTHY!**

You are **MINE!**

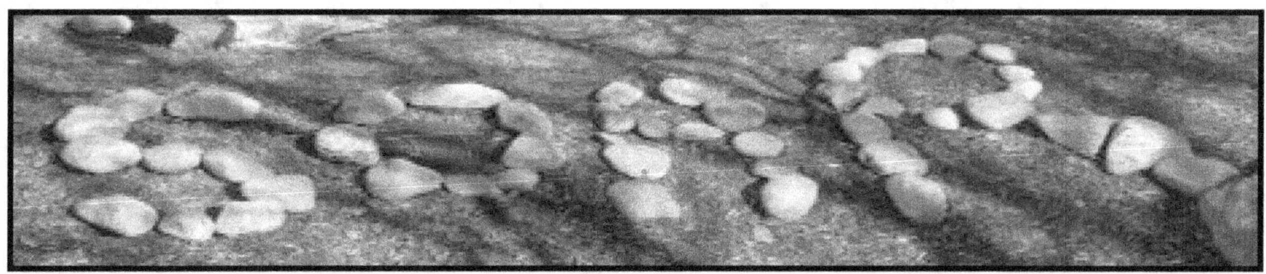

<u>SOAR</u>

Your young mind could only wonder,
Your broken heart could only ponder,
Your bruised feet could only wander.

Days turned into months of praying,
The months turned into years of searching,
You slipped behind a mask afraid of what people
might ask.

Silently you yelled,
Silently you screamed,
Daringly you ROARED! I heard you!

Trust in My timing

No more wanting,
No more wishing,
No more waiting,

You are FREE to be creating all you dream!
Take a leap of faith and unleash your darkest
ROAR!
Now exhale and **SOAR!**

You are capable of moving mountains,
You are worthy of loving,
You are more precious than gold.

Trust in My timing

Your wings- once broken - now healed by Grace!
Spread your wings,
Now exh*ale*, and SOAR!

Trust in My perfect timing

He went before you to open the door,
His love never fades,
His wisdom will always guide you,
His challenges forever shaped you.

All your fears aside,
Be courageous.
You are ready to stand.

You must start SOARING.
You need to be exploringthe great unknowns,
Finding the destiny I your Heavenly Father made
wholly for you!

In loving memory of Jason R. Taylor

Shenandoah National Park in Virginia
The journey is rocky, but the view at the top is worth the climb!

Teach My Heart

Holy is Your name, Lord!

Holy are Your ways, Lord!

Holy is Your heart, Lord!

Holiness is my longing, Lord.

Holiness is my aim, Lord.

Holiness is my call, Lord.

Teach my heart Your perfect ways.

Compassion is Your name, Lord!

Compassion is Your way, Lord!

Compassion is Your heart, Lord!

Compassion is my desire, Lord.

Compassion is my focus, Lord.

Compassion is my love, Lord.

Teach my heart Your perfect ways.

Trust is Your name, Lord!

Trust is Your way, Lord!

Trust is Your heart, Lord!

Trusting is my weakness, Lord.

Trusting is my concern, Lord.

Trusting is my lesson, Lord.

Teach my heart Your perfect ways.

Love is Your name, Lord!

Love is Your way, Lord!

Love is Your heart, Lord!

Love is my brokenness, Lord.

Love is my written language, Lord.

Love is my hope, Lord.

Teach my heart Your perfect ways.

Teach my heart to have Faith,

Teach my heart to have Hope,

Teach my heart to have Love.

Faith, Hope, and Love lead me to adoration.

Faith, Hope, and Love lead me to my future.

Faith, Hope, and Love lead me to freedom

Your perfect way heals my broken heart,

Your perfect way heals my tarnished trust,

Your perfect way heals my tarnished love.

Amen!!

Flying on swings brings me great peace and joy!

I love to soar to the heavens and talk with Jesus!

Where do you go to find childlike joy?

Encouraged

It Is Your Time

Too many voices silenced yours,
Too many lies kept you behind doors,
Too many days you did not have the strength to soar.

Find rest in your mind,
Find rest in your heart,
Find rest in your soul,
You will be whole again.

Let courage shine from the inside out,
Embrace your story to give God the glory,
Be honest and true,
Let others hear your voice.

It is time to open the window to your heart,
It is time to free your dreams,
It is time to experience victory,
It is your time!

Let joy radiate from the inside out,
Embrace the laughter for God's happily ever after,
Be authentic and kind,
Let others feel your love.

It is time to open the window to your soul,
It is time to free your legacy,
It is time to experience resiliency,
It is your time!

YOU are treasured!
YOU are valued!
YOU are loved!
It is time to let it reside within your heart!

READY.....SET....FLY ON THE WINGS OF YOUR STORY!

Where will your dreams and life lessons carry you if you let them?

I AM

I am

Balancing reality and who I want to be,
Redirecting memories to give them less power,
Attending to the darkest grief my heart has ever known,
Vocalizing my deepest needs to people who graciously support me,
Enduring a long and tedious journey to embrace the gift of perfect healing.

I am

Standing on the threshold of fear and hope,
Treading unfamiliar waters to reach a new shore,
Reassuring myself that I'm worthy of healing and being heard,
Outwardly showing I'm not turning back on my goals,
Navigating the lies to learn God's truth,
God's precious and loved child ALWAYS and FOREVER!

I am BRAVE and STRONG!

Finding my strength and facing fears at Adventure Park in Virginia Beach.

<u>You Always Have</u>

You always have imagined this day would come:
  listening to the stories of my classroom,
  watching me living my childhood dream.

You always have known I could rise above the ashes:
  no matter how many times I fell,
  no matter how much I doubted myself.

You always have been proud of me:
  proud for kicking butt in all life's challenges,
  proud for finding my way on a healthy journey.

I cling to your confidence in my abilities:
  I lean on your endless wisdom,
  I soar on our precious memories.

This special day belongs to you as much as it does to me.

Dressed for the commencement ceremony:
  Tears stinging my face,
  I look to the sky above.
  Can you see me?

This special day is dedicated to you!

Days
  Weeks
    Months
      Years
        Decades

You sprinkled my life with laughter, joy, and encouragement.
You pushed me to my breaking point with love.
You waited for me to learn countless life lessons.

Thank you!

*This moment of remembrance is where I felt Jason's nudge
to keep moving forward as he would cheer me on from above.*

Two week after this moment, I registered for a Master's program.

*You Always Have was created as the culmination of the promise
I made him in this prayer while visiting New York City.*

Never Unnoticed

A friendly smile,
A simple wave,
Never unnoticed by my little eyes.

My ears captured by the music,
My timid voice joined the band,
My lonely heart transformed by the lyrics.

A friendly smile,
A simple wave,
A kind nod,
Never unnoticed by my little eyes.

Church became my sweet escape from hate,
Church became my safe refuge from pain,
Church became my secret comfort from fear.

A friendly smile,
A simple wave,
A kind nod,
A gentle hug,
Never forgotten by my hurting heart.

Your name soon replaced only knowing a familiar face,
Your musical talents poured blessings on so many people,
Your presence always uplifted my hidden burdens.

A friendly smile,
A simple wave,
A kind nod,
A gentle hug,
A spoken word of encouragement,
Never forgotten by my hurting heart.

Little did I know you would become my friend for decades,
Little did I know you would become one of my music teachers and mentors,
Little did I know we would be pilgrims together to many Holy places.

A friendly smile,
A simple wave,
A kind nod,
A gentle hug,
A spoken word of encouragement,
A reminder of God's work in my life,
Never taken for granted by my healing soul.

Big dreams were spoken during Steubenville years,
Big mountains were climbed on our own journeys,
Big prayers were answered and victoriously celebrated together.

A friendly smile,
A simple wave,
A kind nod,
A gentle hug,
A spoken word of encouragement,
A reminder of God's work in my life,
A constant rock of faith in my abilities,
Never taken for granted by my healing soul.

Honored to have known you most of my life,
Honored by the gift of your listening ear all these years,
Honored by the impact you have made to help me soar.

A friendly smile,
A simple wave,
A kind nod,
A gentle hug,
A spoken word of encouragement,
A reminder of God's work in my life,

A constant rock of faith in my abilities,
A precious gift of friendship I will forever treasure,
Never overlooked by my overcomer spirit.

You have made a difference!
You have been a powerful beacon of His love!
You have done more than words can begin to say!

A friendly smile,
A simple wave,
A kind nod,
A gentle hug,
A spoken word of encouragement,
A reminder of God's work in my life,
A constant rock of faith in my abilities,
A precious gift of friendship I will forever treasure,
A special blessing to be known and prayed for by you,
Never overlooked by my overcomer spirit.

Thank you for noticing my potential hidden behind the mask of shame,
Thank you for always being there,
Thank you for guiding me to our Lord.

Nothing you, Padre, have done has been unnoticed!

Here I am exploring the streets in Europe.

Where in the world do you want to explore?
I have learned so much about myself with the gift of traveling.

Friendship Reflection

Grace flows through you,
Peace abounds when I'm with you,
Faith surrounds all we do.

Your friendship is a gift,
Your friendship is a reflection of who I'm meant to be,
Your friendship goes deeper than the sea.

Trust pours out freely,
Hope fills our souls,
Love overflows from our cup of Joe's.

Your friendship is a gift,
Your friendships is a reflection of God's work in my soul,
Your friendship makes me feel whole.

Fears fade when we laugh,
Music captures our inner thoughts,
Dreams shine with a twinkle in your eye.

Your friendship is a gift,
Your friendship is a reflection of how far I've come,
Your friendship is a special one!

Gratitude flows through me,
Amazed at all we've shared,
Our friendship reflection has been the Starbucks blend of God's perfection!

Love you, my dear friend!

Struggles will always come and go like crashing waves!

My amazing village of dear friends have taught me to embrace each challenge with courage and not fear.

Stand firm in your faith and allow the struggle to grow you from the inside out!

Unbreakable Bond

You took a chance on a little girl lost in the shadows of fears,
You took a chance wiping away a little girl's hidden tears,
You took a chance investing in a little girl for years.

A bond unbreakable,
A bond irreplaceable,
A bond undeniable.

You taught her how to laugh again,
You taught her how to trust again,
You taught her how to believe again.

A gift unbreakable,
A gift irreplaceable,
A gift undeniable.

You took a chance on a teenager trapped from injustice shattering her core,
You took a chance opening your door to listen to a teenager roar,
You took a chance believing in a teenager's ability to soar.

A mentor unstoppable,
A mentor unmatchable,
A mentor undoubtable .

You raised her spirits,
You raised her hopes,
You raised her confidence.

A teacher unstoppable,
A teacher unmatchable,
A teacher undoubtable.

You took a chance on a young adult yearning for zest,
You took a chance sharing your family with a young adult feeling distressed,
You took a chance assuring a young adult she is blessed.

A hero incomparable,
A hero untouchable,
A hero unforgettable.

You mended her broken heart,
You mended her shattered dreams,
You mended her fragile self-worth.

Heartbroken...

She knelt at your beside,
She knelt at your casket,
Now she is kneeling at your grave.

Thinking.....

The strongest mentor I've ever known,
The kindest teacher I've ever known,
The bravest friend I've ever known,

Has flown on the wings of an angel to his forever home.

Crying....

Farewell my wise mentor,
Farewell my encouraging teacher,
Farewell my wonderful friend.

Smiling....

I will love you forever and always, Jason.
I will love your family forever and always.
I will love because you loved me.

Our bond unbreakable,
Your impact untouchable,
My mentor is unforgettable!

*Thank you to the entire Taylor family for sharing Jason with me
and for all the ways you have blessed my life.*

*This picture holds
a special place in my heart.*

*Jason never let me give up on
my greatest dream of being an educator.*

*Here we are standing
at Kutztown University where
we both earned our teaching degrees!*

*Finding comfort after the loss of a loved one
can be a difficult task.*

*As the months pass without Jason,
I am learning to find the
longed-for hug when sitting on his deck
and sipping coffee from a mug
I gave him years ago.*

*As I sip, I listen to the birds,
I reflect on our memories on the deck,
and I soak up time with his beautiful family.*

Thank you for reading and embarking
on my journey of healing from childhood experiences as I perceived them.

I wish you all the best as you walk your precious life journey.
Please know there are many people in this world
that need to hear your story.
You are worthy to be heard and worthy to be free from harm.

Pouring my soul on paper has been
a meaningful and difficult process.
It has required a village of friends that have
encouraged me, cried with me, and believed in me
when I felt the lies of impossibility.

I pray you find a village that can walk with you and bring you to a place of being free
and sharing your story of being your own champion!

YOU GOT THIS!

Janice Marie has found tremendous joy in her childhood dream
of being an educator.
She currently teaches kindergarten and strives to pass on the legacy
of all the teachers she had in school.

In 2019, Janice Marie presented her graduate research at the annual
Trauma Informed Educators Network conference held in Nashville, TN.
Her goal is to continue encouraging people to share their voice
and be empowered to overcome all adversities.

The journey is rocky, but the view at the top is worth the climb!

In her free time, Janice Marie can be spotted at the local ice-skating rink! She is
an adult member of the United States Figure Skating Association and competes on
a Theatre on Ice team. Joining the skating team has allowed her the opportunity to
keep learning new things and model her own advice of "dream big and never give up!"

Janice Marie is a 2020 United States Figure Skating Association
Get Up Ambassador!

Janice Marie has the honor to wear ice skates
that have been autographed by
Scott Hamilton, 1984 Olympic Champion.